GERTY'S PAPA'S CIVIL WAR

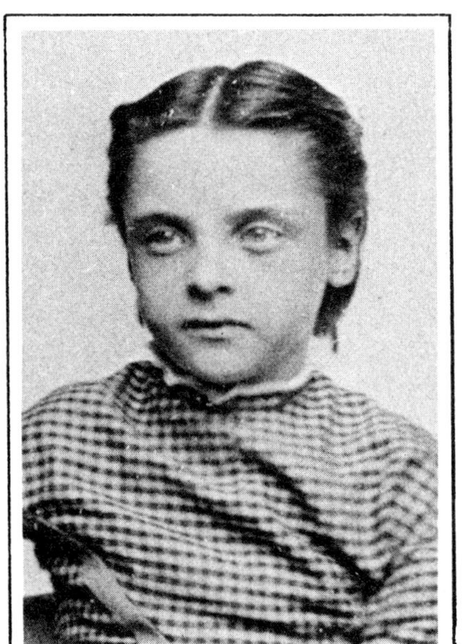

Gerty and her papa

Mary Gertrude Smith

Edward Parmelee Smith

GERTY'S PAPA'S CIVIL WAR

Edward Parmelee Smith

Edited by
William H. Armstrong

THE PILGRIM PRESS
New York

The biblical quotations in this book are from the
King James Version of the Bible.

Library of Congress Cataloging in Publication Data

Smith, Edward Parmelee, 1827–1876.
Gerty's papa's Civil War.

Includes bibliographical references.
1. Smith, Edward Parmelee, 1827–1876—Juvenile literature.
2. Smith, Gerty, b. 1859—Juvenile literature.
3. United States—History—Civil War, 1861–1865—Personal narratives —Juvenile literature.
4. Congregational Churches—United States—Clergy —Biography—Juvenile literature.
I. Smith, Gerty, b. 1859.
II. Armstrong, William H. (William Howard), 1932–
III. Title.
E601.S636 1984 973.7′83′0924 84-1874

ISBN 0-8298-0703-9 (pbk.)

The Pilgrim Press, 132 West 31 Street, New York, NY 10001

Contents

About This Book

This is a book about the Civil War. It is made up of letters written by a man who worked among the soldiers and heard the bugles and the guns. The man sent the letters home to his daughter, Gerty, to tell her what the war was like.

No one person could have seen the whole Civil War, but Gerty's papa saw a great deal of it, in Virginia and Tennessee and Georgia. And he knew how to write about the things he saw so that others could picture them in their minds. To make the picture even clearer, real photographs from Civil War days are included with the letters.

Some of the things Gerty's father wrote about may seem strange. That should not surprise us in letters that are more than a hundred years old. People did things then that are not done today. But that is what makes the letters interesting. They are like a window that lets us see into another time, into Gerty's and her papa's time—the time of the Civil War.

Gerty's real name was Mary Gertrude Smith, but her parents called her Gerty. Her father's name was Edward Parmelee Smith, but his friends called him E.P. and Gerty called him Papa.

Gerty lived with her parents and her younger brother, Clarke, in the little town of Pepperell, in Massachusetts.

Gerty's mother, Hannah Cleaveland Bush Smith.

Gerty.

Gerty's father.

Gerty's brother, Clarke Smith.

The Congregational church in Pepperell, Massachusetts, where Gerty's father was the minister and where Gerty went to Sunday school and church.

Everyone in Pepperell knew the Smiths, because Mr. Smith was the minister of the Congregational church there. In 1859, the year Gerty was born, the church building burned down. But the people soon built a new one, and it was beautiful.

The children of the church loved their minister, and he loved them. He could call each one by name, and whenever he walked down the street, they crowded around him. As he moved along, he usually held a child's hand in each of his. The other children would hold onto his coattails, for in those days all the ministers wore long-tailed coats.

Other ministers talked just to the adults in the Sunday services and sometimes bored the children. But Gerty's father sometimes talked just to the children. When he did that, more people came to church than on other days. He talked in a way the children could understand, and they liked to listen to him. Even the adults liked to listen. One Sunday a woman asked for a copy of his talk because she liked it so much. He thought she meant his sermon to the adults. But no, she didn't want that—she wanted a copy of his talk to the children!

Gerty's father had two nieces in a nearby town whom he enjoyed visiting. They liked to play with him, and one day they braided his hair into little pigtails, all over his head, and tied them with bits of cloth. The pigtail that hung over his forehead they tied with a red, white, and blue ribbon. When the Smiths started for home, Gerty's mother said, "Edward, you had better unbraid your hair, or you will forget and go somewhere that way."

"Oh, no," he said. "I'm going right home."

And he did. But while he was unharnessing the horse, he remembered that he needed to see one of the leaders of the village and he went to visit him—braids and all. When he got home, Gerty's mother said, "Edward, where have you been?"

"To see Mr. B———."

"Look in the glass."

After he looked in the mirror and saw his braids, Gerty's father said, "I thought Mr. B——— looked at me in a strange way. In fact, he kept on looking at me the whole time we talked."

Gerty's father just laughed about the trouble his nieces had gotten him into.

But Gerty's papa had a serious side too. A war was going on between the northern states and the southern states. The southern states wanted to leave the Union and make their own country, and the northern states wanted to stop them from leaving. Many young men from Pepperell and from other Massachusetts towns had gone to fight in the war. Some had been killed or wounded. The hospitals were full, and there were not enough ministers in the army to visit the sick and the wounded or to bury the dead. Gerty's father decided that he would go to the army to be a minister to the soldiers.

A group of people called the Christian Commission was sending ministers to the army and offered to send Gerty's father too. He asked the church members if he could go, and they said yes. The next day he got on a train and went to Virginia, where many of the northern soldiers were.

It was hard for him to be away from Gerty and Clarke; Gerty was just four years old, and Clarke was two. It was hard for him to be away from the other children in Pepperell too. There were so many new things to tell them, things he had seen in the army: steamboats and railroads, drummers and buglers, captains and generals, army horses and army tents. He could not talk to them in church now, but he could write to them. So he wrote letters to Gerty—at least they were addressed to her—but he meant them for all the children. He had the letters printed in a children's magazine called *The Well-Spring*. That way thousands of children could read them and learn about the Civil War.

Gerty and her Papa are gone now, but the letters are still here. I found them in some dusty old copies of *The Well-Spring*. I enjoyed reading them, and I think you will too.

William H. Armstrong

VOL. XX. BOSTON, OCTOBER 9, 1863. NO. 41.

PUBLISHED BY THE MASSACHUSETTS SABBATH SCHOOL SOCIETY, BOSTON.

NEW AND SPLENDID PICTURES.

WE have before informed our readers, that Mr. ORANGE JUDD, — the editor of one of the best and most widely circulated agricultural journals in the country, The *American Agriculturist*, is also a practical Sabbath-school man. He is interested not only in the training of trees and vines, and all manner of plants and shrubs, and all kinds of domestic animals, but also in the training of children. He gives them a prominent place in every number of his journal, so that, in the seventy-five or one hundred thousand families where the *Agriculturist* pays its monthly visits, all the children give it a hearty welcome. To make it attractive and useful to them, he illustrates every number with splendid pictures, which he has had engraved at great expense, expressly for his work.

On account of his great interest in the young, Mr. Judd has kindly consented to an arrangement, — our readers will be pleased to learn, — by which we can have the use of quite a number of his finest illustrations.

The above fine picture is one of them.

Every reader can see what this engraving represents. "Scenes like this," says the editor, "are now common in all parts of the loyal States. You see the soldier has been wounded in the leg, and is now

The cover of a wartime issue of *The Well-Spring*, the magazine that printed the letters Gerty received from her father.

Two Civil War photographers, with their camera on a stand at the left of the picture.

A Word About the Pictures in This Book

Gerty's father did not take a camera with him to the army. Not many people had cameras in those days, and the ones they did have were heavy and hard to use. But a few people did take cameras to the war and photographed many of the same things and the same people Gerty's father saw and wrote about. Some of their pictures are included in this book so you can see how the things you are reading about really looked.

GERTY'S LETTERS FROM HER PAPA IN THE ARMY

* *1* *

My House Is Made of White Cloth

Falmouth Station, Virginia.

My dear little Gertrude:

Would you like a letter from Papa tonight? I wish you could come into my house and bring your brother, Clarke, and Mamma with you.

My house is made of white cloth. You could not ring the bell or rap on the door, but you would draw your finger down the side of my house where it opens as if you were scratching it, and I should say:

"Who is there?" and you would say:

"A little girl."

"What does the little girl want?"

"She wants to see her papa"; and then I should jump up and untie the strings and catch Gerty in my arms and give her ten kisses, five on each cheek. And then I should say, "Gerty, won't you take a chair?" You would look at me and say:

"Why, Papa, that is not a chair—that is only a box."

"Well, my little girl, that is all the chair I have. Gerty, have you been to tea?"

"No, sir." "Come, then, and we will have some." You would say:

An army tent.

"Why, Papa, where is the tablecloth? What funny plates and teacups! only cups like Clarke's mug. Where are the cakes?"

"Papa doesn't have cakes."

"Where is the butter?"

"Mary* has not sent Papa any."

"And no cheese? no meat? I wonder where you found such a supper."

After supper Papa would take you on his knee and sing "John Brown's Glory." Then you would kneel down on the ground—because Papa has no carpet and no floor to his house—and say your prayers. Then Papa would say, "Now, Gerty, it is time to go to bed." You would begin to unhook your dress and untie your shoes. "Oh, no, that is not the way in my house. We never take off our clothes to go to bed, but put on more." Then I should wrap you in a nice warm blanket and lay you down on a board to sleep.

Pretty soon you would hear the drums go *rub-a-dub-dub.* That means for the soldiers to go to bed. Then something would go *toot, toot.* That is the way the rebels† tell their soldiers to go to bed. Then you would shut your eyes and go to sleep and *dream.*

At prayers in the morning I want you to say this verse: "It is a good thing to give thanks unto the Lord." And then you can have it for your Sabbath-school verse. Good-bye.

From your Papa in the army.

*Mary was probably a woman who worked for the Smiths in Pepperell.
†Many people in the northern states called the soldiers from the southern states "rebels." They were also called "Confederates."

A drummer boy.

A bugler. Drums and bugles were used to tell the soldiers what to do.

* 2 *
A Hospital Is a Place for Sick Soldiers

My dear little Gerty:

Your Papa is on a steamboat and going from Belle Plain to Aquia, in Virginia. It is a bright morning, and the Potomac River is as smooth and shining as your Mamma's looking glass.

Over on that shore, just beyond those oxen, you see some white houses. They are soldiers' houses. They call them tents. They are made of cloth, stretched over a pole and tied down with ropes. Do you remember your verse for Sabbath school? "How amiable are thy tabernacles, O Lord of hosts"? The tabernacle was the Hebrews' meetinghouse, made of cloth, stretched by cords and stakes.

Well, Gerty, these tents that I was going to talk to you about are for a hospital—Windmill Point Hospital. There are a great many of them, more than you could count on all the fingers and toes you have, and all those in your house. A hospital is a place for sick soldiers. If Mamma and Clarke and Mary and Aunty Shipley* should all be sick, and the doctor should bring some beds of straw and lay them in the front room, he would call that room the hospital for our house.

In the army the soldiers get sick from cold or fever or

*Aunty Shipley was a neighbor of the Smiths in Pepperell.

Steamboats at Aquia Creek Landing, Virginia.

An army hospital in Virginia.

wounds from the rebel guns, and they have to go to the hospital. When I came to the army, a few weeks ago, those tents were full of sick men. I did not see one little girl or boy there. Sometimes a mother would come to see her sick soldier boy.

One day a lady came from Pennsylvania. She had heard that her boy was sick. She asked the doctor about him. He told her to sit down, and he would go and see. He went and looked into the soldiers' hospital tent, and they were just tying up the soldier's face. He had died only a few minutes before! The mother fell down on the ground when the doctor told her and cried and cried as if her heart would break. "Oh my boy, my boy! Why didn't you keep him, Doctor, till I could come?"

One day a soldier boy, about as large as Johnny Farrar,* sent for someone to come and pray for him. I went into his tent. He said, "I cannot get well. Write to my mother and tell her I am not afraid to die, that I want to go home once more very much to see her and my sisters. I am all the brother they have. But it seems that God wants me to die in the hospital, and God knows best about it. Tell my sisters to be sure and come to me in heaven. Tell my mother that I am not sorry that I came to be a soldier."

I took my Testament from my pocket and read what Jesus said about the mansions in his Father's house and that verse that Gerty learned, "God shall wipe away all tears from their eyes," and then Papa prayed for the soldier, who folded his hands and tried to pray too. When I arose from my knees he said, "Oh, that is good. That is the way my mother used to pray with me. Come again." I carried him a pillow and some clean sheets, and some handkerchiefs that some little girl had sent to the soldiers. He smiled so sweetly when he said, "Thank you," that it was worth all the ride from Massachusetts to look on his face.

Now, all the soldiers have been taken away from Windmill Point Hospital, and this boy—if he is living— was carried to

*Johnny Farrar was a sixteen-year-old boy who lived with the Smiths in Pepperell.

another in the city of Washington. Nearly all the sick soldiers were carried to other hospitals in the army. Papa slept in one of them last night. When it was time to go to bed, I said:

"Soldiers, some of you have family prayers at home before you go to bed. Would you like to have us read out of the Bible and pray with you?"

"That is right," "That's good," "I like that," they said. So I read, "The Lord is my shepherd," and then we sang "Going Home to Die No More." And Mr. Bullard prayed for us all—for the soldiers, for the fathers and the mothers and all the children at home, and then for the sick men lying on their blankets.

This Mr. Bullard is not the children's Mr. Bullard,* but his nephew, Henry, who has come from Andover to give the soldiers Testaments and books and Sabbath-school papers, and talk with them about Jesus and pray with them.

[A small part of the letter is missing here.]

Now, Gerty, save your *Well-Springs*. Thank God every day that you have so nice a paper, that you are not a sick soldier, away off here without your mother and father, and pray God to bless the soldiers and keep them from being sick and help them not to be wicked.

Perhaps I will tell you, in my next letter, about Lizzie Scott and her loaf of bread.

Papa.

*"The children's Mr. Bullard" was Asa Bullard, editor of *The Well-Spring*.

Henry Bullard, who prayed for the soldiers and their families.

* 3 *
Lizzie Scott and Her Loaf of Bread

My dear little Gerty:

Would you like to hear about Lizzie Scott and her loaf of bread? Two weeks ago I was in the tent of the Christian Commission at Falmouth on a cold, dark, stormy night. The wind was blowing hard, and the snow was coming down in little round, hard balls, like those you have heard patter against the window. We were thinking of rolling ourselves up for the night when two men came in helping another, whom they called Captain. They said he had been wounded, was sick, and unable to walk to his regiment without supper.

We made him some hot coffee and gave him a loaf of bread. The loaf was wrapped in a paper and had a letter pinned on it. The captain opened it and found it was from a little girl in Philadelphia whose name is Lizzie Scott. She had heard one of the Christian Commission tell of some sick soldiers who cried when they saw a loaf of bread, and she cried too when she heard it and ran to ask her mother if she could give something for the soldiers.

Her mother said, "Yes, my dear," and Lizzie brought all her pennies and asked her mother to make a loaf of bread and write a letter for her. Her mother made the bread—a nice round loaf—then wrote what Lizzie told her to the soldier.

Tents and ministers of the Christian Commission.

Lizzie, you know, is a little bit of a girl, only six years old, and couldn't write, but she could think and talk, and her mother's fingers would put her think and talk on the paper, and that would make a letter. So the bread and the letter both came to this sick captain. He read the letter first, and then he let me see it, and if you would like to hear it, I will tell you exactly what was in it.

Dear sick Soldier:

I send you a loaf of bread which I bought of my mother with my pocket money. I hope you are not very sick. Perhaps you have no little girl, but you have had a dear mother who took care of you when you were a little baby boy, and if she is alive, I know she prays for you. Don't forget her; and when you are going to do naughty, think how it would make her feel. It must be hard to be good in the army. Shall I call you my soldier, and pray for you every day?

Good-bye, dear soldier; may God bless you, I pray.

Lizzie Scott.

The captain took out his handkerchief and wiped his eyes, and said Lizzie was a dear little girl, and he would write to her and thank her for the bread, and tell her to call him her soldier, and pray every day for him.

What do you say, Gerty, would you not like to be like Lizzie and do something to help the soldiers?

When the ladies at the sewing circle send the next barrel, you can put in your *Well-Springs* and *Child at Home** and some of your pennies. No matter if they all go; and then, when you lie down on your soft warm bed, close beside your little baby brother, remember the soldier who stands up and walks about all night with a gun in his hand, or lies down on his blanket in the wet and cold and gets sick and has to be

**Child at Home* was another magazine.

An army captain.

carried to the hospital; and ask God to help us drive the rebels back and to bless little Clarke's flag, the *Stars and Stripes*, and Gerty's flag, the "ed, white and boo," so that the war will be over and the hospital tents taken down, and the soldiers come home to see their mothers and go to Sunday school.

Papa.

* 4 *
A Soldier Boy Who Is Going to Die

Papa's tent, Belle Plain, Virginia.
Wednesday night, March 11, 1863.
Almost blanket time.

My dear little Gerty:

Papa has been running about among the soldiers all day carrying books and Sabbath-school papers. He has a black bag, which the soldiers call a haversack, that hangs by his side with a strap over his neck.* In this bag he puts nice Testaments, little hymnbooks, and papers and then takes a large bundle of papers on his arm and goes marching off in the mud. The mud is so deep that Gerty could not walk in it and Clarke's little fat legs would stick fast, and I should lose my boy if he should try to walk here.

Papa goes about among the soldiers' houses, little houses (some of them so small that Gerty and Clarke could hardly stand up in them), and lifts up the cloth door and calls out:

"Boys, would you like something to read today?" Some soldiers say:

"I haven't any money." Then Papa says:

"I don't want any money. I came to *give* them to you."

*One of the men in the picture on page 15 is carrying a haversack.

“Oh, yes, that’s good.” “Thank you, sir. Now Jim, we’ll have something to read.”

“Have you a *Testament,* boys?” One says:

“Yes, I have one that I got at Sabbath school.” Another says, “I have a *Bible* that Mother gave me.” Another says, “I lost mine when we were fighting the rebels in Fredericksburg and haven’t had any since.”

Then Papa goes on farther to another soldiers’ house and then another and another and another and so to a great many; and then he goes across the field to another place where the soldiers’ houses are. He sees something lying on the ground. It is a horse. Perhaps he is asleep—no, he is dead. Here is another dead horse. There is a dead man. There is a broken wagon.

Then come the soldiers, with their packs on their backs and their guns. They are going to drill—march up and down and back—and run, just as Gerty saw them do at Groton one day.

Then Papa goes over to the hospital where he used to sleep. One man is dead. He had a fever. They have wrapped him up in his blanket and are going to bury him. The drums go *rub-a-dub* and the whistle blows, and the soldiers march with their guns bottom upwards, down to the soldiers’ graveyard. They put the coffin down by the grave and stand up in a row. Papa takes off his cap, and takes out his New Testament, and reads about the mansions that Jesus has in his Father’s house and about dying and how God shall wipe all tears from their eyes.

Then we sing out of our little hymnbook, and Papa prays for these men that are all going to die and for the dead man’s little children who will never see their father again till they all go home to die no more. Then Papa talks to the soldiers and tells them to be good soldiers, and say their prayers, and love their mothers, and love God, and try hard every day to do what God wants them to, so that when they die, they can go and live with God. Then Papa steps back, and the man at the head of the line says to the soldiers:

“Load at will”; and the soldiers put some noisy powder in their guns, and the man says, “Ready! Fire!” Bang! go all the

Dead horses and broken wagons.

Soldiers drilling.

Soldiers who have gone to a graveyard to bury the dead.

guns, just like the cannon that made Gerty cry one day at the post office.

The drum goes *rub-a-dub* again, and we all march back.

Papa goes to the hospital, and there's a soldier boy who is going to die. He doesn't know it, but the doctor has told Papa that he can't ever get better and *perhaps* won't live to hear the birds sing in the morning. Then Papa goes softly to the soldier's bed—takes his hand and smooths his hair and forehead.

"How do you do, tonight, my dear fellow?"

"Not quite so well—can't breathe easy."

"Do you think you are going to get well again?"

"I don't know."

"Well, are you all ready to get well or to die?"

"I don't think I am."

"Do you love Jesus?"

"I try to."

"Do you ask him to forgive you?"

"Oh, yes, a great many, *many* times. I want you to pray for me."

So Papa kneels down, and the soldier folds his hands, and we pray that if the soldier lives, he may be a good boy, and if he dies before the birds sing in the morning, he may go to hear little children and angels sing in heaven. Good night, dear soldier: Papa must go away off to his tent. In the morning perhaps the doctor will send for Papa to come to the soldier's funeral. Papa has just written a letter to the soldier's mother to tell her how sick her boy is and that perhaps when the next letter comes he will be *dead*.

Now, good night, my dear Gerty; kiss everybody for Papa, and tell them he is coming home as soon as he can leave the soldiers.

Papa.

* 5 *
Help Make the Soldiers Happy, and "Ragged Rebels Ashamed"

Gerty belonged to the Sunday school at Pepperell—or the Sabbath school as they called it. Once when her father wrote, he wrote to the other members of the Sunday school as well as to Gerty.

* * *

Army of the Potomac.
March 16, 1863.

To my dear Sabbath school:

Among the good things which I have been permitted to distribute to the soldiers have come some pretty little bags such as I used to call a "work bag," but now I call them "little comforts." The dictionary name is "housewives."

It seems that the Sabbath-school children in Albany united, and on a given Sabbath each scholar brought a bag to her class. The superintendents collected them, and on Monday, when they came to count them, they found 5,000 ready to go. They came in boxes to the Christian Commission at Washington and have been given out one by one to the soldiers in this army. If you could see their faces when I hand out a bag and

A box for the soldiers, outside the Christian Commission office in Washington.

say, "Boys, do you want any needles, pins, thread, and buttons? Some little Sabbath-school girl made that for you and sent it to me to give to you." "To *give* to us? Bully for you! A *new kind of sutler,** boys!" "See here, Jim, if a fellow goes ragged after this he's a *bummer.*" (That's a soldier's name for loafer.) "Sabbath-school girls, eh? Those are great little girls; they don't forget the boys gone a-soldiering." "I used to go to Sunday school." "That's where I belong." "I have got a little girl in Sunday school; wonder if she did not have a hand in one of these bags." So they talk till I am out of sight. Some of them pull out the tract† and some find a letter in the bag and read it aloud. The news that Vicksburg is taken does not waken up a more lively, pleasant feeling among the men than a quantity of those bags freely given.

I read some of the letters. Here is one, as nearly as I can remember it:

> *Dear Soldier:*
>
> *It must be hard for you to keep your clothes nice, so far away that your mother cannot come to mend them; so I send you this bag of needles and thread, and you can mend for yourself. I would send a thimble, but Mother says you could not use it. Now I hope you will keep your clothes very nice, so that when the ragged rebels see you they will be ashamed of themselves.*
>
> *We talk about you, and pray about you in the Sunday-school concert, and every night I pray "God bless the soldier!" Good-bye, soldier.*
>
> *From your young friend,*
> *Hattie.*

I'll warrant that soldier will put that letter in his Testament and carry it home with him, if he lives to go home.

Now I want to ask you to do as the Albany children have

*A sutler was someone who followed the army to sell things to the soldiers.
†A tract is a religious paper.

done, and on the second Sabbath in April each of you, old and young, boys and girls, bring a comfort bag to your class. Put in two kinds of buttons, three or four needles, two kinds of thread, one linen, two rows of pins, and a tract or soldier's book, and a *letter* to the soldier. Say a few words to him, just as you would to a friend you knew and loved. If you cannot write, get someone to write your words for you, but let them be *your* words.

If you have no tracts, your superintendent or your pastor will have some ready for you. Come now, children, help make the soldiers happy, and "ragged rebels ashamed."

From your pastor, who never goes to sleep without praying for you.

Edward P. Smith.

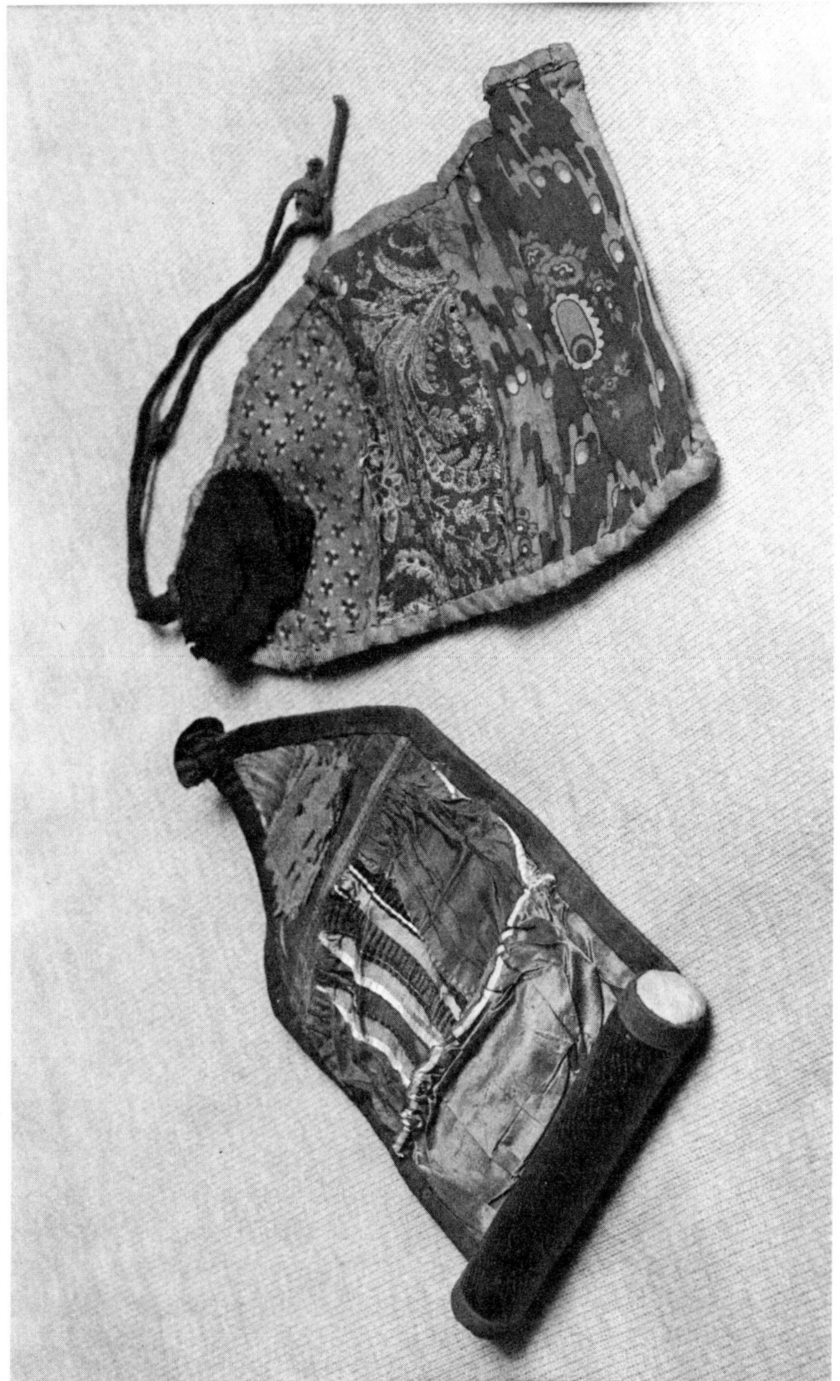

Comfort bags carried by two soldiers from Ohio during the Civil War.

Not all the Confederate soldiers whom Hattie and Gerty's father called "ragged rebels" were really ragged, but these two were nearly in rags when they were captured in Virginia.

* *6* *
He Is Just Like These Leaves

Belle Plain, Virginia.
March 19, 1863.

My dear little Gerty:

Yesterday, when your Papa was at breakfast in his cloth house, eating pudding and codfish, a soldier rode up to the tent and said, "Is Mr. Smith, Christian Commissioner, in?" "Yes, here he is." "I have a telegraph letter* for you."

Papa opened it. "Is Philip yet alive? Answer immediately." Papa hurried up his pudding, put on his coat, took off his nightcap and put on his shiny cap, and walked fast over to the hospital, and looked in where Philip used to lie, and he was *gone!* Papa asked the nurse, "Where is Philip?" "He's dead and buried, sir!"

So Papa wrote a letter to send by telegraph wire, which they call a telegram, and told his father: "Philip was buried last Sunday."

Then I went down to the bank of a little brook and found a new grave. There was a board standing in the ground by the grave marked *Philip Hutchins*. Close by the head of the

*A telegraph letter is a letter sent in code over electric wires and then written out so it can be read; this kind of letter is also called a telegram.

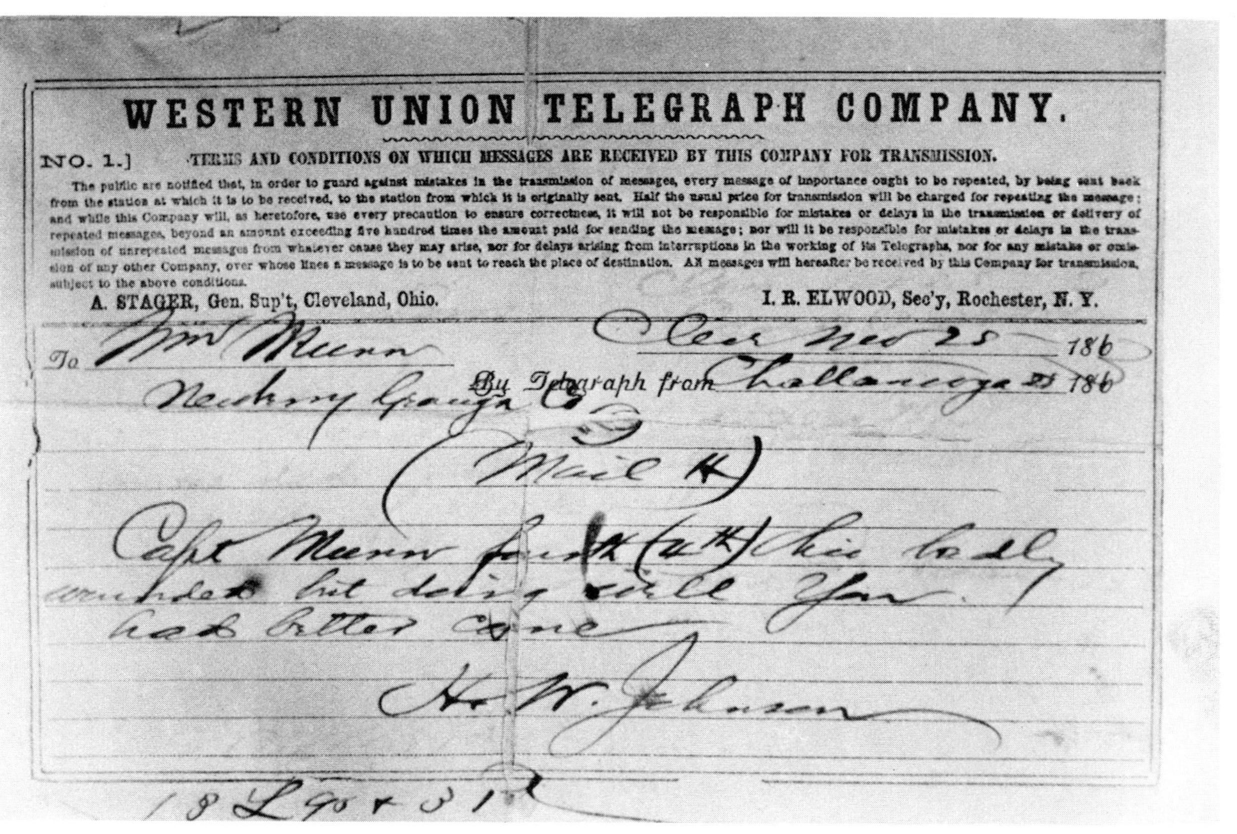

WESTERN UNION TELEGRAPH COMPANY.

NO. 1.] TERMS AND CONDITIONS ON WHICH MESSAGES ARE RECEIVED BY THIS COMPANY FOR TRANSMISSION.

The public are notified that, in order to guard against mistakes in the transmission of messages, every message of importance ought to be repeated, by being sent back from the station at which it is to be received, to the station from which it is originally sent. Half the usual price for transmission will be charged for repeating the message; and while this Company will, as heretofore, use every precaution to ensure correctness, it will not be responsible for mistakes or delays in the transmission or delivery of repeated messages, beyond an amount exceeding five hundred times the amount paid for sending the message; nor will it be responsible for mistakes or delays in the transmission of unrepeated messages from whatever cause they may arise, nor for delays arising from interruptions in the working of its Telegraphs, nor for any mistake or omission of any other Company, over whose lines a message is to be sent to reach the place of destination. All messages will hereafter be received by this Company for transmission, subject to the above conditions.

A. STAGER, Gen. Sup't, Cleveland, Ohio. I. R. ELWOOD, Sec'y, Rochester, N. Y.

To Wm Mann Nov 25 186

By Telegraph from Chattanooga 186

A telegram sent to the family of a wounded soldier.

A lone grave under a tree.

grave was a beautiful live oak tree. Papa picked two leaves from the tree and put them in another letter and sent them through the post office to his mother. And when she gets them, she will put them in the big Bible and keep them very carefully; and always when she sees them, she will say, "My dear boy, Philip, is dead! He is just like these leaves. His face is all faded; there is no light in his eyes; his hands can't move." But that is only his body. His soul—and that was Philip himself—that used to move those hands and look out of those eyes and listen at those ears has gone home to die no more. And his mother, if she loves God as Philip did, will go and live with him; and his father will come too, and they will have a new house in heaven—one of the mansions that Jesus says he has all ready for everybody that loves him. When Philip's mother thinks of this, she will be happy again—as happy as a mother can be who has heard that her only boy is dead and buried in Virginia, and she could not go to see him when he was sick and could not go to his funeral or look for once on his face.

But when the rebels are all driven away by our guns and swords and the soldiers have come home from the war, then, perhaps, Philip's mother will come down to Belle Plain and find this grave, with the board marked "Philip" right by the live oak tree. Perhaps she will bring a nice white stone like those we see in our graveyard and put it up where the board is. And then, when she grows old and wants Philip to take care of her and make her happy, she will keep thinking of her boy that went to war and died in Virginia; and very often, if you should look in her face, you would see a tear dropping off her cheek and running down on her hand. But then she will say, "Philip was a good boy. He loved his mother. He asked for her the night he died. He gave himself to Jesus too. He loved the Stars and Stripes and went to war to help save his country. And now the country is saved, and everybody is happy except those poor old mothers like me who have lost their dear boys; and I will be happy too, for Jesus will take care of me, and pretty soon I shall go home where Philip is, to die no more."

Don't you think, Gerty, that all boys ought to be good to their mothers? What do you think little girls should be? That is a question from

Papa.

Belle Plain, Virginia.

* 7 *
Are You Not Glad That You Are Not a Sick Soldier, Away Out in Virginia?

My dear little Gerty:

Papa is riding on a steamboat this morning from Belle Plain to Aquia. He has only this bit of paper to write Gerty a letter.

Last night Papa slept on his blanket in a white cloth house, and when he woke up this morning the birds were singing beautifully. A little red bird sat up in a high tree and opened his mouth and sang, oh, so *sweetly!* Then a large brown mockingbird* jumped up over red bird's head and sang just like him. Then red bird sang again. And mockingbird sang again, when red bird flew away. I suppose he thought mockingbird was saucy.

When the birds were gone, Papa went into one of the white houses, where there were a great many sick men—more than Gerty's fingers on both hands. One boy was trying to read a book with a red cover. His hand trembled, his head ached, and his lips were all sore and dry. He was very pale and tired and sick. Papa looked into his book. It was a little Bible. His sister Jane gave it to him. Papa asked him if he loved his Bible.

*The mockingbird is found mostly in the southern states. It can imitate or mock the sounds of other birds.

A wartime steamboat.

"Very much."
"Do you love Jesus too?"
"Oh, yes, yes, and I want to hear you pray."
So Papa knelt down on the ground and asked God to bless this poor sick soldier and make him very patient and help him to get well, so that he could go home and see his sister and his mother.
The other sick soldiers listened, and some of them got out of bed and knelt down. Some of them cried and asked me to come again.
Now, Gerty, are you not glad that you are not a sick soldier, away out in Virginia?

From your dear
Papa.

Two months after Gerty's father had gone to Virginia the Christian Commission asked him to go to Tennessee and talk with the generals there to see if they would allow ministers to work in their armies too. After Gerty's papa got the generals' permission, he was put in charge of the ministers who came to work with the soldiers.

Tennessee was a southern state and one that had left the Union. Many of its people were fighting against the Union soldiers. But Papa found that some people in Tennessee still loved the Union. Soon he was writing to Gerty to tell her about these people and about the fighting in Tennessee.

* * *

* *8* *

His Mother Would Have Called Him Union

Winchester, Tennessee.
August 12, 1863.

My dear little Gerty:

I want to tell you about the people in Tennessee. They are a strange kind of people. The little children never sing "Red, White, and Blue," nor say, "Hurrah for 'tars and 'tipes," as Clarke does. They never pray, "God bless Yankee Doodle, and the soldiers of the Union"*; but they hate the flag, and if they see it, they want to pull it down and stamp on it; and when they see a Union soldier with a blue coat, they want to kill him. A little bit of a boy whose name is Aaron told me I was a Yankee. "How do you know, little boy?" "'Cause you wear a blue coat." "Do you like Yankees?" "No, I hate Yankees." Aaron has a brother who is a rebel soldier, and he says he is going to have a gun pretty soon to shoot a Yankee with.

But there are some of these people in Tennessee that love the flag and cried when they saw it pulled down. They can't say, "Hurrah for the flag of the Union!" as you do, because the rebels would shoot them; but they keep thinking, "Hurrah," all the time; and by and by, when the Union soldiers get way down here with guns and swords enough, they will make the rebels run, and then the people can swing their hats and

*Soldiers of the Union were soldiers from the northern states. They were also called Yankees or bluecoats (because they wore blue uniforms).

flags, and the boys and girls can clap their hands and sing "Red, White, and Blue" and "John Brown's Body" too. These rebels have been very wicked and cruel. They ride right up to a house and ask the children, "Where is your father?" "He is gone," the children say. "Where is your mother? Tell her to come out." Then the mother comes out softly. She is afraid they are going to hurt her children. "Where is your old man?" "He is gone away." "You needn't tell us that story; we know where he is—he is in the Yankee army. Where is your oldest boy?" "He has gone too." Then they swear at the woman, and drive off her cow and mule, and catch her chickens, and take her corn, and shoot her pigs, and sometimes they burn the house. Then the poor woman takes her baby in her arms and leads one little boy and the older sister leads two more, and they go off wandering about, nobody knows where. When it comes night, they may have to lie down in the woods. Perhaps they won't get any breakfast.

Papa saw a poor old woman who had been driven out of her house by the rebels because she told them she had a boy in the Union army with his father, and she wished her little Tommy was big enough to go in too. They stole everything she had and burned her house. She started off at night with seven children to find the Union soldiers. A good man who lived near took six of the children into his house and took care of them. But the mother could not leave her little white-haired baby boy. She wrapped him up in her old shawl as well as she could and came on foot a long, long way, twice as far as from Gerty's house to where Charlie Boston lives. She kept her baby snug in her arms, and when she was tired and her arms ached, she would sit down on a log and lay her boy in her lap and sometimes go to sleep holding him. When she came to a house, she asked for milk for the baby and some biscuit and meat. Sometimes they would give her some, and sometimes they asked her where she was going and why she didn't stay at home; and when she told them her house was burned up because she and her children and their father loved the Union, they would drive her away and make her sleep

The ruins of houses burned by soldiers during the war.

outdoors all night without any supper.

When Papa saw this poor woman, she was all tired out. Her clothes were worn and ragged and [her] shoes nearly all gone. Her little baby was very poor. She said he was not so heavy in her arms as he was when she started from her burning

Richard W. Johnson, the general who became angry because of the way a woman had been treated.

house. The poor little thing was almost worn out. It was too weak and sick to laugh and could hardly cry.

The mother brought her babe to General Johnson and sat down on his piazza.* He is a Union soldier, and the President [Abraham Lincoln] likes him so well and thinks he is so good a soldier that he has given him two little silver stars, and the General wears them one on each shoulder.

He asked the woman what she wanted, and she told him all about how the rebels drove her off and burned her house, and some of the people on the road would not give her any supper or bed for her baby because she loved the Union. Then the General was angry. He shut his great hand tight up and brought it down hard on the railing and said, with a naughty word—which I wish he had left out—that he loved the Union better every day he lived because he saw how wicked the people were who were trying to break it in pieces. Then he took his pencil and wrote word to the conductor to let that woman go on the cars† when she wanted to; and he called a soldier—the soldier's name was "Orderly"—and told him to find a house for the woman to sleep in and to get her something to eat.The mother cried and took up her boy and kissed him, and left some little teardrops on his cheek, and thanked the General, and told him God would love him, and went over to the house.

The next morning Papa went to see her. She was walking in the room. Her eyes were red, and she had no baby in her arms. "How is the little one this morning?" Papa asked. She shook her head and her chin quivered, and then she threw her apron over her face and cried right out. Then Papa knew the baby was dead. The women in the house said it died in the night, and they buried it early in the morning. They had no coffin, and so they took a box that used to have soldiers' bread in it and put the baby in it in the grave which a soldier dug. The mother cried and cried, and Papa tried to tell her how Jesus loves little children and sometimes he wants them so

*A piazza is a porch.

†This is another way of saying "on the train" (the railroad cars).

much to come and live with him in heaven that he sends down an angel and asks some mother if she won't let her little boy and girl come and live with him. A great many mothers have sent their babes away, and now Jesus has this little East Tennessee boy that was not old enough to have a name, close by his side in heaven. And Jesus will give him a pretty name. I wonder what it will be. If he had lived, I think his mother would have called him Union.

Now, Gerty, when you kneel down to say your prayers, you will not forget to ask God to bless this poor crying mother and all her other children, and their papa and brother in the army, and bless General Rosecrans and help him to take his soldiers with their blue coats and their horses and guns and swords and cannon straight over the mountains into East Tennessee, where these good people live who love the Union, and scare away all the naughty rebels. If God helps General Rosecrans, he certainly will do it. And if all the praying boys and girls ask God to help him, I think he will.

Papa.

After Gerty's father had been with the army a whole year, his family traveled by railroad and steamboat to join him in Nashville, Tennessee. Gerty's mother was soon busy keeping house for the many ministers who came to work among the soldiers. She also cooked for the soldiers in the army hospitals in Nashville.

Gerty was five years old now, and sometimes she went with her mother to take soup to the wounded soldiers. To see a mother and a little girl in the army hospitals did the soldiers good, and they enjoyed the special food that was brought to them.

One day Gerty's mother took her pails and tubs

General William S. Rosecrans.

and baskets of food and went among the soldiers on their hospital cots. A soldier, who was badly wounded in the shoulder, tried to be brave and said he did not need any special food. He did not even want any chicken soup. But when he saw the blackberries Gerty's father had bought and sent along, his courage gave way. He took some, and when the sugar was sprinkled on, he cried out, "Sugar too! and white sugar at that! That's too much," and he had to ask the nurse to wipe away his tears. The next day the soldier's cot was empty. The blackberries had been the last gift anyone had given him.

Many other soldiers were in the hospitals because they were sick. Three-year-old Clarke became sick with the same fever the soldiers had, and a short time later he died. His parents knew that they too might get sick if they stayed among the soldiers, but they never gave a thought to leaving. They sent Clarke's body back to Massachusetts to be buried in the Pepperell graveyard, but they stayed in Nashville. The soldiers needed them.

Gerty's papa continued to write to Gerty when he traveled among the soldiers. He no longer needed to write about some things; Gerty could see soldiers and hospitals all around her in Nashville. But her father found new things to write about as he visited soldiers in other places, like Atlanta, in Georgia.

* * *

Sick and wounded soldiers in an army hospital.

* 9 *
Would You Like to Go to Atlanta?

My dear little Gerty:

Would you like to go to Atlanta? Well, we will start from Nashville this afternoon. You will find it a long, long ride. The cars only go twelve miles an hour, and it is three hundred miles.

You know where the depot is at Nashville—right under the hill, close by Hospital No. 14.

It is a noisy place. There are more engines than you can count on all your fingers twice over. Almost two hundred cars go out of this depot every day.

What do you suppose they have in them? Pork and crackers, and corn and oats and hay, and gunpowder and minié balls and shell and cannon shot.*

Do you know what all these are for? The soldiers eat the pork and crackers. They call them sowbelly and hardtack. The corn and oats and hay are for the horses and mules; and very glad they will be to get them all along the way; and if any of these bags of corn should get as far as Atlanta, the

***Minié balls* were the kind of bullets the soldiers used; *shells* were shot out of guns and then exploded; *cannon shot* was what the soldiers would shoot out of a cannon.

The railroad depot at Nashville, Tennessee.

mules will be so glad to see them that they will eat up the bags and all.

The powder and iron balls and minié balls are to be put into the guns and cannon; and when rebels come in sight of our soldiers, they will try to shoot them with one of those little minieś or one of those great long iron shot, which has some powder inside of it which will make it fly to pieces, or one of those heavy round shot, which you could roll on the floor but could not lift. A great many rebels have been hit with shot like these, and they have hit a great many of our soldiers with their shot. That is what makes so many men lying in the hospital and so many walking about the streets on crutches or with their arms tied up. That is what makes so many ladies at church wear black bonnets and dresses. Their papa or brother or husband or son has been hit with one of those hard balls, and he was killed right off; or the soldiers laid him on a piece of canvas-cloth that is nailed to two sticks, which they call a "stretcher," and carried him to the ambulance; and the driver took him to the hospital, where he died.

If you will look at those cars which have just come in, you will see the wounded men getting out. They have just come in from Chattanooga; and a few days ago they came from Atlanta. They were hit with the rebels' shot when they were trying to get into Atlanta to drive the rebels out, and they have been suffering and lying in hospital ever since. Now they have a furlough.

Do you know what that is? The doctor comes and looks at that man's leg. It has a large sore on it, where one of the rebel minié balls was cut out. He takes a piece of paper and writes on it: "This soldier is unfit for duty for thirty days," which means that he will be all that time getting well before he can take his knapsack and go "marching on." The doctor sends this paper to the brigadier general, the man with a silver star on his shoulder, and he writes on it: "This man can go home and see his mother and little children, if he will come back in thirty days." That is his *furlough.* Every soldier is glad to get one, because then he can go straight home; but if

Soldiers learning how to carry the wounded on stretchers and how to put them on an ambulance.

he should try to go without a furlough, another soldier with a gun would say to him, as he was getting into the cars, "Where are your papers?" which means, "Who told you you could go home?" and then, if he shows him this paper from the doctor and the general, he can go; but if he has no paper, he can't go. That paper is his furlough.

But he must take care and come back when his paper says. His mother must not keep him too long, and his little boy must let him go again so as to be in Nashville before the thirty days are all gone. If he is sick or lame, it makes no difference; if he can ride on the cars, he must go. Do you see how glad all those soldiers look? They have that paper in their coat pocket; and they are thinking about home all the time and wondering who will be at the depot to meet them when they get there and whose little feet will be running down to

Wounded soldiers riding on railroad cars.

open the gate for them.

But you must hurry now, little girl, or you will not get on the Chattanooga train.*

Do you see that log house on wheels, right on the track

*The train from Nashville to Atlanta went through Chattanooga, Tennessee.

To all whom it may Concern.

Extract from Army Regulations, edition 1861.

Par. 190.. Furloughs will be granted only by the commanding officer of the post, or the commanding officer of the regiment actually quartered with it. *Furloughs may be prohibited at the discretion of the officer in command.*

Par. 191.. Soldiers on furlough shall not take with them their arms or accoutrements.

The bearer hereof, Daniel Whaley Private of Captain Geo. D. Sponsors Company of the 6th Regiment of New York Artillery aged 25 years, five feet Eight inches high, Sandy complexion, dark eyes, ~~Sandy~~ hair, and by profession a Farmer; born in the Town of New Fairfield, and enlisted at Patterson Putnam Co in the State of New York on the 12th day of September eighteen hundred and Sixty two, to serve for the period of 3 Years, is hereby permitted to go to New Fairfield, in the County of Fairfield, State of Connecticut, he having received a **FURLOUGH** from the 17th day of January 64 to the 27th day of January 64 at which period he will rejoin his Company or regiment at Camp Near Brandy Station Va or wherever it then may be, OR BE CONSIDERED A DESERTER.

Subsistence has been furnished to said Daniel Whaley, to the 9th day of January 1864 and pay to the 31st day of October 1863 both inclusive.

Given under my hand, at Camp Hunt near Brandy Station, this 15th day of January, 1864.

A A Crookston
Major
Commanding the Reg't.

[A. G. O. No. 90 & 91.]

A furlough given to a soldier named Daniel Whaley.

behind the engine? That is full of soldiers. They look out of those holes, and if any rebels come, they run out their guns and shoot at them. The logs are so thick and strong that the rebels cannot shoot through to hit them. All these cars are full of meat and crackers.

"Dear me! See the soldiers climb up on top of the cars! Are they going to ride up there all the afternoon and all night? Won't they fall off when they get asleep and the cars go rattling along?"

Yes, they have to ride outside, because inside it is full of barrels and boxes. Sometimes a soldier falls off, if he has been drinking bad whiskey, but hundreds and sometimes thousands go that way, and they get through very well.

Some of these soldiers have been home on a furlough, and some of them have been in hospital and are going back to camp. The doctor calls them *convalescents*. Do you know what that means? When a sick man has got almost well, they call him a convalescent. It will be cold tonight on top of the cars for these almost-well soldiers. You see, some of them have no blankets; they can't get any till they get where their captain is. Some of them have no overcoats; they could not carry them in the summer, when it was so hot marching in Georgia, and so they threw them away. Now, if we could go up to the Christian Commission and get some mittens, wouldn't they be nice and warm for these cold fingers that have to hold on to the car all night?

There, Gerty, don't you hear? One of the convalescents speaks to you. He is coming down. Never mind now; he will not hurt you. No soldier who takes a little girl in his arms that way is going to hurt her. Do you know why he wanted to take you? He has a little girl—you may depend upon it—way up in Michigan, and when he saw you, it made him think of his little Susy or Nelly, and he couldn't stay up on the cars. Do you feel that little wet spot on your cheek, close to where he kissed you? I wonder if it can be a tear? Do papas ever cry when they think of their little girls?

There goes the bell! See the soldiers jump up now! That is

not our train. They don't put girls on the top of the cars; and they don't let them go anyway, unless they have a *pass* from the general.

Do you know what a pass is? The general takes a piece of paper and writes: "Guards and pickets* and military conductor, pass this man to Chattanooga," which means, "Let him go, soldiers; and if he wants to go on the cars, let him ride for nothing."

Sometimes there are so many soldiers and officers that there is no room for girls or anybody else who does not carry a gun or sword. Here is our train, right on behind the other, loaded full inside with bags and barrels and outside with soldiers, all except that last car. That is a regular passenger car, with seats in it.

Now if we can get in. What a crowd! That soldier with a gun, at the door, will not let you go in till you ask the captain standing right at the steps. The captain looks at everybody's pass to see if the general has said they may go. Then, if the cars are not full and all the soldiers that have straps on their shoulders have gone in, you can go.

But don't you see the cars are full now? And here are some more soldiers with straps. That lady that has gone in and is sitting at the window will have to come out, because here is a

*Pickets were soldiers set out around an army to guard against surprise attacks.

Office Provost Marshal, Harper's Ferry, Va. May 23

Guards and pickets will pass Thomas Ott

to Halltown **Good for** one **days**

Description—Age **height** **complexion**

eyes **hair**

Residence Jeff co **Captain and Provost Marshal.**

By order of Brig. Gen. Max Weber, Comd'g.

[AC 3919]

A pass given to a person named Thomas Ott.

soldier with a silver eagle on his shoulder, and he must have that seat.

Well, Gerty, it is pretty certain we shall not go to Chattanooga today. Do you see, some of the officers can't get on, because the car is full? That is pretty bad, because they ought to be in Chattanooga. It may be their general wants them there, but now they will have to go back to the St. Cloud Hotel and give four dollars apiece to stay there till the next train goes tomorrow.

These are officers. Do you know what that is? It is a soldier who carries a sword and has a strap—not a leather strap, but a short strap of cloth worked with gold thread and sewed on to the coat—on each shoulder. The lieutenants' and captains' straps are very much alike. The colonel has an eagle in silver thread worked in his strap. A general, that they call a brigadier and sometimes brig, has one silver star worked in his strap. A major general has two stars in his strap, and

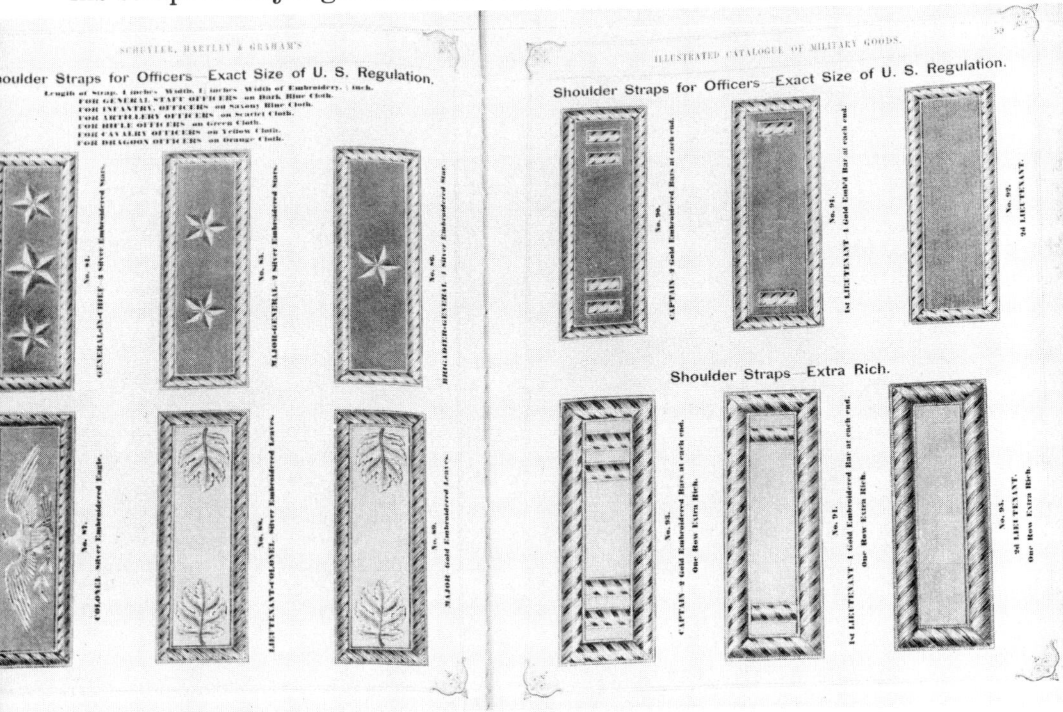

An old catalog showing the shoulder straps that Union officers could buy to sew on their uniforms.

Ulysses S. Grant wearing the three stars of a lieutenant general on his shoulder straps.

General Grant, the only lieutenant general there is, has three stars. They call the soldiers' doctor, Surgeon, and sometimes they call him Major, because he has a major's strap—a leaf worked in gold thread. Which of all the straps do you like best? I don't know which the children would choose, but I suppose almost all the soldiers think that *three stars* make the prettiest strap. Do you know why?

Hear the soldiers hurrah as the cars go off! They are almost always full of fun. I wonder if that is why we call them *boys?*

That woman who is wiping her face with her apron is an East Tennessean. That was her boy on the train, with a cavalryman's coat on. Do you know what a cavalryman is? A soldier who rides on a horse and carries a kind of sword that they call a saber and has a yellow binding on his coat.

That mother is afraid she will never see her boy again. How many of all these soldiers, Gerty, piled on top of those cars will ever come back again to this depot? I don't know, but I am sure there are a great many mothers and little sisters who would like to be here to bid them "good-bye."

That other tall woman, in a calico dress, without any hoops, is from Mississippi, the state where Jeff Davis* used to live. She has come all the way with her daughter, in a wagon, to Nashville. She wanted very much to get on the cars, but there was not room. Do you see how pale she is and how sorrowful she looks? Something is the matter with her, and when I tell you what it is, you will not wonder that she cries.

You remember the prison over near Dr. Franc's Hospital—that large stone house with a high wall all around it? It is full of little rooms, not one of them big enough for Aunty Lawrence's† bedstead to go in. They call these rooms *cells*. The walls to the rooms are stone, and the floor is stone, and the door is iron and has a stout bolt and padlock. In one of these cells is a full-grown boy, as large as the largest man in Pepperell, twenty years old. He is a rebel lieutenant and has been

*Jefferson Davis was the President of the Confederate States of America, the government of the southern states during the Civil War.
†Aunty Lawrence was a neighbor of the Smiths in Pepperell.

A company of cavalrymen from Pennsylvania.

shut up here since last March. They call him a "rebel prisoner," that is, a rebel shut up in prison. But they do not shut all prisoners up in stone cells. This man has to go in here because he is a bad rebel—a guerrilla.

Is not that a hard word? See if you can pronounce it. You need not stare at me so. I know what you are thinking about, little brown eyes. You are going to ask me what a guerrilla is, and that is just what I was going to tell you. He is a rebel who pretends to be a soldier but does not stay with the rebel army. He hides about in the woods, and when he gets a chance, he steals a horse or cow from any man who loves the Union, or breaks into his house and gets his money, and sometimes kills the Union man, and burns his house, and drives his children off cold and hungry. And when he thinks a Union soldier is coming along the road, he hides in the bushes till the soldier gets close up, when *whack* goes a gun and the soldier is shot dead! Then the guerrilla jumps up and snatches the soldier's porte-monnaie* and hat and boots and runs off to the bushes again. Sometimes they call this guerrilla a bushwhacker. Do you know why?

This rebel, bushwhacking guerrilla in the stone room is the youngest boy of that crying mother in the depot. Shouldn't you think she would cry? I am afraid the poor thing will cry harder yet before many days, for it is an awful thing to be a guerrilla and shoot Union soldiers. But we cannot stop now to talk with her. We shall see her again sometime, and then we shall know what is to become of her boy. It will be of no use for us to come down here tomorrow. We must wait till the hospital cars are going to Chattanooga, and I am pretty sure the medical director (he is the head doctor) will let us ride in his cars.

Papa.

*A porte-monnaie is a small purse.

Three Confederate prisoners.

A guerrilla named Champ Ferguson in prison at Nashville, Tennessee.

When the war was almost over, the Christian Commission asked Gerty's father to go back to Virginia. He went, but he was in Virginia only a short time before the Commission asked him to go to Philadelphia, in Pennsylvania, where the Commission had its office. From his desk in the office, Gerty's father helped send ministers and books and comfort bags to the soldiers in the whole country. He worked in Philadelphia until the war was over.

Gerty's mother did not go to Virginia or to Philadelphia. She and Gerty stayed in Nashville. Nashville was still full of soldiers and hospitals, and as long as there were sick and wounded soldiers who needed help, they would not leave. Four months after the war was over they finally left, to be with Papa and to take a rest.

* * *

GERTY'S LETTERS FROM HER PAPA AFTER THE WAR

During the war, President Abraham Lincoln freed the slaves who lived in the southern states. When the war was over the freed slaves, or freedmen as they were called, wanted more than anything else to go to school and learn to read. Gerty's father decided to help them just as he had helped the soldiers during the war. He went to work for a group called the American Missionary Association, which built schools in the South and sent teachers to teach the freedmen. He visited many northern towns, looking for teachers who would help. One of the towns he visited was Oberlin, in Ohio. And, of course, he wrote to Gerty to tell her about Oberlin.

* * *

* 10 *
That Is the Way They Do Things at Oberlin

Oberlin, Ohio.
October 1, 1865.

My dear little Gerty:

I have been to church and Sabbath school in this beautiful town today and seen a great crowd of children and young folks and old folks. The Sabbath-school room was full, and the infant class was full, and the church was full. I talked to the children about Jesus and his love for very little folks and about the two birds in the tree who sang to the little boy that was asleep under the tree. Do you remember what the birds said? Then I talked to the Sabbath-school children about the army and the good soldiers who died in hospitals at Nashville and other places.

In the church, President Finney preached—an old man, and a great man, and a good man. He began to preach when he was young and has been preaching ever since; I suppose as many as fifty years. He has preached every Sabbath except when he was sick, and sometimes every day in the week.

There is a large college in Oberlin for young men and young women and a large school for boys and girls. There are more than seven hundred young people here at school and college.

Charles Grandison Finney, president of Oberlin College, Oberlin, Ohio.

Mr. Finney has been president of the college a long time. He has talked to the students and preached to them and prayed for them; and a great many more than you know how to count have become good men and good women, and they have gone to teach other schools and colleges all over the country. Many of them are going to Tennessee and Mississippi and other states at the South to teach the colored people and preach to them.

Now, can you tell, Gerty, *why* the Oberlin young men and women go down South more than other scholars? If Gerty had been to church with me today and to the Sabbath school, and if you had gone into the college with me yesterday, you would know why. You would see white boys, and boys almost white, and boys almost black, and boys black enough for anybody, sitting on the same seat or walking together to school. And you would see girls with brown hair, and girls with black hair and long curls, and girls with black hair and short curls—so short that you could not make a waterfall* of them—and with black eyes and black cheeks, sitting close together, reciting and singing together, and praying together. In the students' prayer meeting, a black student speaks and prays just as well as a white one. They all pray together, just as if they were all of one color.

But I was going to tell you about the colored people here. Everybody is kind to them. They don't call them "niggers" any more, but "colored people," and sometimes "colored ladies" and "colored gentlemen." They don't keep them only to cook in the kitchen, and black boots, and take care of horses, but the colored people have houses of their own, and horses and pianos, and send their children to school, and have white people to work for them. Just across the street from where I am writing, there lives a Negro woman—no, I forgot, a colored lady—and she has a white woman to help do her kitchen work! Wouldn't that seem strange in Nashville and a little bit strange in Boston? Well, that is the way they do things at Oberlin. President Finney tells all the scholars, and

*A waterfall is hair arranged in long, loose waves.

Some of the students at Oberlin College in 1865.

the other teachers are all the time telling the scholars, that a white man is just as good as a black man, if he behaves as well, and that no white man has any right to think that there is any good in his color. You might as well say that a girl with black eyes is not as good as a girl with gray eyes, as that a girl with black cheeks is not as good as a girl with rosy cheeks.

Now, don't you see *why* the scholars at Oberlin should be all ready to go South to teach the Negroes? Some of these teachers are Negroes themselves, going back to the country they ran away from to help teach their brothers and sisters and other colored children. Many of them are white teachers who have learned at Oberlin to pity and love everybody that is poor and wants to learn how to read and be better. And so they go right away, as soon as they hear that these colored people in Virginia and Georgia want to go to school, and take a Testament and hymnbook and spelling book, and find a room, and call the children in; and sometimes their fathers and mothers and uncles and aunts and grandfathers come too, and they have a school. Do you know what kind of a school that is? You will see something about it in your *Well-Spring.* It is a *school for freedmen.* Eight lady teachers are going from Oberlin tomorrow down the Mississippi River to teach such schools. The American Missionary Association sends them on the cars and the steamboat and gives them money to buy clothes and food. Do you know where the American Missionary Association gets the money to give these teachers? If you don't know, ask Mamma to tell you about it.

I heard something today about a little colored Sabbath-school girl that made me laugh. She had a verse to say. It was the seventh verse of the third chapter of the First Epistle of John. Get your Testament, and let Mamma read it to you.* This little girl remembered what it meant but had forgotten how to say it. So, when her teacher called her, she stood up, and said:

"'Little children, let no man fool you.'"

*1 John 3:7 says, "Little children, let no man deceive you."

A school for freedmen somewhere in the South.

That was like the colored boy at Natchez, Mississippi, where so much had been said about marrying, since the slaves have been set free, because their weddings, when they were slaves, were not of the right kind. This boy's verse was in the fifteenth of John. He stood up and said it:

"'I am the true vine, and my father is a married man.'"*

The white children may laugh at these little colored folks for a while, but it will not be long before our very best Sabbath schools will be among the Negroes.

Let us have schools for all the colored children and help them to be wise and good.

Papa.

*John 15:1 says, "I am the true vine, and my Father is the husbandman." A "husbandman" is a farmer. The boy confused the word with "husband," which is a married man.

Some people in the South did not like the freedmen and did not like the teachers who came from the North to teach them. One year after the war, some of the people in Memphis, Tennessee began to shoot the freedmen and burn their houses and schools. Gerty's father hurried to Memphis to see what had happened and then described the trouble to Gerty in a letter. He knew Gerty would want to know what was happening to the freedmen like those she had seen in Nashville during the war.

* * *

* *11* *

Dreadful Days to the Colored People of Memphis

Memphis, Tennessee.
May 14, 1866.

My dear little Gerty:

Would you like to get a letter from Memphis? I am sure you have been thinking about the colored children in this city ever since the 3d of May, when the *Gazette*, which the man with a bundle under his arm throws into our yard every morning, told us there was a Negro riot in Memphis and that the people were shooting each other on the streets, and setting houses and churches and schoolhouses on fire, and sometimes driving women and children out of their houses and then setting the fire, and sometimes fastening them in the house and leaving them to get out the best way they could while the house was burning up.

I am sure that, while you have heard all these things read in the morning paper, you have been thinking about the colored children and wondering whether any of them were hurt, and whether they will have their churches and schoolhouses again.

I am sorry to say some of them were badly wounded; and some were killed by the bad white people who hate them because they are black and have been slaves.

One colored woman was shot while lying in bed with her babe. A boy was shot dead while crossing the street, not thinking of harming anybody or that anybody wanted to hurt him. Another little boy ran under his mother's bed and hid, but the mob found him and knocked him down with a club and shot him. Nearly one hundred persons were shot: about thirty of them were killed and others are dying of wounds.

All this time—the greater part of two days—the Negroes were doing nothing but trying to get away.

They were not fighting or even defending themselves, but running and hiding; and white men and boys were clubbing and beating and shooting them, breaking open their houses, and robbing them of their money, and, whenever they liked, burning the houses over their heads.

Tuesday and Wednesday, the 1st and 2d of May, were dreadful days to the colored people of Memphis, but Wednesday night the most fearful of all. A large number of their houses were burned, and all their schoolhouses and churches. Some of the churches were large, fine buildings built by the savings of the colored people when they were slaves. There were thirty teachers here, and all had as many scholars as they could teach; I suppose about two thousand five hundred.

Thursday morning there was only one schoolhouse left. These bad men, who hate colored people, are especially angry about their education. They say all manner of bad things about the Yankee teachers and were very glad to be able to break up the schools by burning the houses.

Do you know anything of Lincoln Chapel? I suppose not. It was not a very remarkable building, except to a few colored children, who thought it was the best—if not the greatest—house ever built. Rev. Mr. Tade, who was sent here by the American Missionary Association to help the colored people and to teach their children, built it with his own money—all he had—and some that he borrowed. He built it too with his own hands, and tugged away upon it in the wet and cold of winter till it was done, and then named it after President Lin-

Sketch of an angry mob burning a freedmen's schoolhouse in Memphis, Tennessee.

coln, the best friend the colored people ever had. Here they had their day school and Sabbath school and were as happy a company of little folks as you ever saw. They learned to read very rapidly—much faster than a little white girl that I know. The bad men, who hate Negro schools, hated Lincoln Chapel and burned it with all the other schoolhouses.

In the morning, as soon as it was day, the Missionary and Mrs. Tade went over to see whether the chapel was standing. They found only the ashes and smoking sticks and a crowd of children and grown-up people standing around. They were the Lincoln Chapel Sabbath-school children. Some of them were crying, and so were their fathers and mothers, because their church and schoolhouse was burned down.

You know the Sabbath-school children of Pepperell, Massachusetts, sent some hymns to Lincoln Chapel Sabbath school, but before the hymns reached Memphis, the chapel was burned.

Last Sabbath, I preached to the children in a large college building, and we sang those hymns. I wish you could have heard them. I used to think the Pepperell children were among the best singers in the world, but somehow these colored children seemed to sing more sweetly than any I ever heard before. In two Sabbaths more, they will learn the eighteen hymns on that sheet, and they will be singing in the streets and in their little huts, "Jesus Loves Me," "Something to Do in Heaven," and "Jesus Paid It All." And a great many people will stop to listen and will say what I said yesterday:

"Nobody but the angels can sing as sweetly as good children."

There is one thing more I want to do for the Lincoln [Chapel] Sabbath-school children. Can you guess what it is? Do you know what is the nicest paper for children? I want to send them one hundred copies of that paper every week for a year. How can it be done? I don't know, indeed. You haven't money enough to send more than one paper; and I don't know as you would like to give all that; would you?

I'll tell you what I will do: I will write to Mr. Bullard, who lives in Boston and makes *The Well-Spring* and knows ever so many children in Massachusetts and other places, and I will ask him to tell the children that these colored children in Memphis want his paper. And I think the Sabbath-school children will say, "They shall have *The Well-Spring* every week, and we will find the money."

When Mr. Bullard writes me what they say about this, I will write you again and perhaps will send you the letter which the Pepperell children are going to write to the Memphis children.

Now, good-bye, Gerty! I wonder if you will pray for the colored children. I asked Katy, a few days ago, if she would not pray for them every night, and she said, No, she wouldn't pray *every* night, but she would tell Jesus all about the colored children once, and then he would "'member 'em" every night. Katy was right: Jesus will remember the little children every night; but then he likes to have Katy and all other children remember them every night too and ask him to bless them.

Papa.

Gerty and her father a few years after the war.

Conclusion

Edward Smith liked to help people. After he had helped the soldiers in the war and the freedmen in the South, he began to help the Indians. President Ulysses S. Grant sent him to help the Chippewa Indians who lived in Minnesota. Later the President asked him to come to Washington to work with all the Indians in the whole country. When he left that work he was asked to be the president of Howard University, a school for freedmen in Washington, DC. Then he visited Africa to see about starting schools there. While he was in Africa he became sick and died. He was buried in Nigeria, at a place called Old Calabar.

Gerty was only seventeen when her father died, but she never forgot him. She was proud of him and all that he had done for other people. She liked to think of him as "a friend to God's poor."

Gerty, Ruth, and Gerty's mother many years after the events in this book.

When Gerty grew up
she had a little girl named Ruth
and this book is dedicated to her memory:
Ruth Crawford Mitchell

A Word to Parents, Teachers, and Other Adult Readers

What a surprise to find one of those austere New England divines of old writing for children in such a simple and pleasant way! The unsmiling portraits and heavy books of theology have misled us—at least about this one. The letters this Congregational minister wrote to his young daughter at the time of the Civil War are a delight to read. They are full of charm, wit, and pathos and should delight the young reader as well as the old.

The letters can entertain, but they can do more than that; they can provide today's young readers with a good introduction to the Civil War. Here are the soldiers' tents and insignia, the military railroads and ammunition, the generals and the prisoners described in terms equally well suited for the nineteenth- or the twentieth-century child. Here too in a more somber vein are the hospitals and the burial details, the wounded and the dead. The letters capture both the fascination and the horror of the Civil War, and of war itself.

The letters can also serve a further purpose: to introduce a child to the strange, new world of the past. It has been said that "the past is a foreign country: they do things differently there."[1] The truth of that statement is apparent here. The weapons of war, the passions of the belligerents, the forms of worship are not those of the twentieth century. But that is part of their value. Just as a traveler learns from what is different in a new place, the reader of history learns from what is different in the past, especially if the past is depicted as vividly as it is in these letters.

The young reader traveling through the past may need an adult guide. One who serves as such a guide may find the following comments useful in helping young readers learn and profit from the new things they encounter in this book.

The Civil War

Gerty's father was merely writing about his own experiences in the war, but his experiences were typical and his letters provide a good introduction to some of the major themes of the war.

The suffering was overwhelming. By November 1864 the North had 190 hospitals, with 120,521 beds.[2] Nashville, where the Smiths lived during part of the war, was full of hospitals. Her father casually reminds Gerty where the railroad depot in Nashville is, "close by Hospital No. 14." Disease claimed even more of the men than bullets; five men died of disease for every two who died of wounds.[3] Smith's dwelling on sickness and death is not out of morbid fascination with them, nor is it simply because his role as a minister took him into the hospitals and to the graves. Hospitals and graveyards were the great realities of the war.

Civilian response to the suffering was also overwhelming. The comfort bags Smith asked the children to send to the soldiers were sent by the thousands, and that was but one way in which the children helped. They also made shirts, undershirts, towels, handkerchiefs, checkerboards, crutches, and puzzles, raising money for their projects by picking berries, doing needlework, and holding festivals.[4] The adults responded too; $5,500,000 in cash and goods was contributed to the Christian Commission during the war, and some 5,000 Christian Commission delegates—mostly ministers—went to the field as Edward Smith and Henry Bullard did.[5]

The letters are an accurate guide to other aspects of the war as well. The supply trains that went from Nashville to Atlanta were a major factor in the victories of Sherman's army. The refugees coming from East Tennessee and the guerrilla warfare Smith described to Gerty were common occurrences in the western field of war. Every field of the war had its graves marked with boards and its soldiers hungry for something to read, to say nothing of its swearing generals. The furloughs, the passes, and the shoulder straps Smith described were familiar to every veteran. And the photographs that accompany the letters help the young reader visualize the war with an accuracy even the original readers could not achieve.

One can visit past events only through the eyes of a person who was there. In this case, Smith's eyes saw a great deal and his pen recorded it faithfully.

God and War

Edward Smith's eyes were, to be sure, northern eyes. The Congregational churches were almost entirely in the North, and most Congregational ministers detested slavery and gave their wholehearted support to the Union. Smith was but one of many ministers who urged their people to "ask God to bless . . . General Rosecrans and help him to take his soldiers with their blue coats and their horses and guns and swords and cannon . . . and scare away all the naughty rebels." His letters are not the bland and balanced reflections of the historian, but the passionate views of one entirely committed to the Union.

Just as many ministers were praying for the southern troops. One Confederate said that "the clergy have done more for the success of our cause, than any other class. . . . Not even the bayonets have done more."[6] Young readers will readily see how strongly people felt about the war. What they might be helped to see is the moral ambiguity of the war and the difficulty of identifying God's purposes with those of either the North or the South. Abraham Lincoln stated that ambiguity well in his second inaugural address.

> *Both read the same Bible, and pray to the same God; and each invokes His aid against the other. It may seem strange that any men should dare to ask a just God's assistance in wringing their bread from the sweat of other men's faces; but let us judge not that we be not judged. The prayers of both could not be answered; that of neither has been answered fully. The Almighty has His own purposes.*[7]

The Changing Forms of Religion

In the same way, adults may be able to help young readers understand the religious beliefs and practices of Smith's letters, which may be different from their own. In the letters, heaven is a literal reality and the undoubted place of future reunions with families and fellow believers. God is thought of in strictly masculine terms. Prayers are prayed on bended knees by adults as well as children. Jesus rather than God is the focus of prayer and devotion. And it is Jesus who loves children so much that he sometimes "sends down an angel and asks some mother if she won't let her little boy and girl come and live with him."

That kind of piety was not the product of an extravagant emotionalism or an untutored mind. Gerty's father was a graduate of Yale University and had studied at three leading theological seminaries—Yale, Andover, and Union in New York City. His piety represents the studied convictions of Christians who lived in a different time and did things differently.

Children, however, may be more open to learning about new forms of devotion than adults and may profit by being permitted simply to observe the past at prayer without too much comment or direction. When the child raises questions, it may be enough merely to explain the differences between the beliefs and practices in the letters and those the child knows, without passing judgment on the past.

The Relations Between the Races

After the Civil War, Edward Parmelee Smith was a leader in one of the most notable movements of the nineteenth century, the crusade to educate the freed slaves. Smith and the American Missionary Association, which employed him, were determined to give an education to as many former slaves as possible and to treat them liberally in the process. But what seemed liberal then may seem in some ways illiberal today.

Smith speaks of the freed slaves in terms that some people may find old-fashioned and others may find offensive; they are "colored people" or "Negroes" rather than "blacks," the term that is preferred today. Times change and preferences change. Terms that one generation accepts, another may regard as quaint or insensitive or insulting. However they are perceived today, the terms Smith used were commonly used by liberal-minded people in his generation.

Smith also appears to be unfair in laughing at some children who could not recite their Bible verses correctly. To expect a youthful reader to distinguish a "husband" from a "husbandman" seems as unfair then as it would be today. But the northerners who went South to teach the blacks had high educational standards. Smith expects that Gerty and the other readers of *The Well-Spring* will be able to distinguish between the two words and will see the humor in the mistake, and he was devoting himself to giving the black children of the South an education just as good as Gerty's so that in time they might laugh at such mistakes too.

Death

Perhaps the greatest contrast between Gerty's time and our own is the openness with which Smith speaks about death. He describes a burial detail taking a dead soldier "wrapped . . . up in his blanket" to his grave and on another occasion describes the hospital attendants "tying up [a] soldier's face" minutes after he had died. He relates his conversation with "a soldier boy who is going to die," who "*perhaps* won't live to hear the birds sing in the morning." When he speaks of Philip Hutchins he does not describe him as having "passed on" or "fallen asleep"; he is "dead and buried." Yet with all his frankness, Smith describes death in a natural, easy way as one who had himself come to terms with it.

Death was no secret to Gerty or to most children of her time. Churches in smaller communities had their graveyards nearby, and Smith could write to Gerty about "our graveyard," where she had probably seen him help bury the dead of Pepperell. Many families had seen a baby die, although few of the dead were buried in crackerboxes, like the baby from East Tennessee, or shipped home to the graveyard by express, as was Gerty's brother, Clarke. Gerty and the other children who lived through the Civil War were familiar with death and did not have to be told why "so many ladies at church wear black bonnets and dresses," the traditional signs of mourning.

Twentieth-century children, so often exposed only to the make-believe death of television, may need help in dealing with the presence of death in these letters. They have seen death enacted, but they may never have experienced its reality. To the extent that they can identify with the events in the letters, they may begin to understand that death happens to real persons. At the same time they may also learn that one's religion can be of great help at the time of death. Their curiosity about the accounts of death and burial in the letters may facilitate discussions about death and burial today. Possibly today's children may be more open to hearing and speaking about death than today's adults, who were often shielded from death in their own childhood. Conversations between adult and young readers about the deaths described in the letters may be useful to both ages.

"The Past Is a Foreign Country: They Do Things Differently There"

The opportunity for children to travel, with adult guides prepared to help them interpret new sights and sounds, can be a rich educational experience, especially if the adults are open to ways of living that are different from their own and have no need to impose their ways on others. The opportunity for children to travel back in time, with adult guides who will not stand in judgment of the past but will merely help to place it in perspective, can be no less educational. And Gerty's letters from her papa provide a pleasant place to begin.

Notes

1. L.P. Hartley, *The Go-Between* (New York: Stein and Day, 1980), p. 3.
2. William Quentin Maxwell, *Lincoln's Fifth Wheel: The Political History of the United States Sanitary Commission* (New York: Longmans, Green and Co., 1956), p. 195.
3. Ibid., p. 71.
4. Robert Lester Reynolds, "Benevolence on the Home Front in Massachusetts During the Civil War" (Ph.D. diss., Boston University Graduate School, 1970), pp. 83–88, 264–65.
5. James O. Henry, "The United States Christian Commission in the Civil War," *Civil War History*, Vol. 6 (1960), pp. 381, 387.
6. James W. Silver, *Confederate Morale and Church Propaganda* (New York: W.W. Norton & Co., 1967), p. 96.
7. Roy P. Basler, *The Collected Works of Abraham Lincoln* (New Brunswick, NJ: Rutgers University Press, 1953), 8:333.

Sources

The letters in this book originally appeared in the following issues of *The Well-Spring*, a publication of the Massachusetts Sabbath School Society:

1863: March 27; April 3, 10, and 24; July 3, 10, and 24; October 2
1865: January 13, 20, and 27; December 15 and 22
1866: June 22

The letters have been rearranged in the book to present them in the order in which they appear to have been written. Some of the spelling and punctuation in the letters has been modernized.

The Congregational Library in Boston, Massachusetts, contains the collection of *The Well-Spring* from which the letters were taken.

PICTURE CREDITS

THE PICTURES IN THIS BOOK ARE USED BY THE COURTESY OF:

The Amistad Research Center, New Orleans, Louisiana: frontispiece (both pictures); ix; xi; 78; 81

Cleveland Public Library, Cleveland, Ohio: 75 (from *Harper's Weekly*, May 26, 1866)

Congregational Library, Boston, Massachusetts: xv

Geauga County Historical Society, Burton, Ohio: 29; 32

Library of Congress, Washington, DC:
  Manuscript Division: 54; 56;
  Prints and Photographs Division: 26; 33; 42; 52; 62

National Archives and Records Service, Washington, DC: viii; x; 13; 17; 71

Oberlin College Archives, Oberlin, Ohio: 67; 69

Beatrice B. Parker, Pepperell, Massachusetts: xii

Herb Peck Jr., Nashville, TN: 63

U.S. Army Military History Institute, Carlisle Barracks, Pennsylvania:
  Military Order of the Loyal Legion of the United States, Massachusetts Commandery: xvi; 4; 9; 10; 15; 21; 22; 30; 36; 38; 43; 46; 48; 53; 58; 60
  Francis A. Lord Collection: 6
  USAMHI: 7

Vermont Historical Society, Montpelier, Vermont: 23

Western Reserve Historical Society, Cleveland, Ohio: 50; 57